A
History of Alresford

derived from manuscript notes by ROBERT BOYES,
Master of Perin's Grammar School in 1774

BY

A. J. ROBERTSON

formerly Rector of Alresford and
Hon. Canon of Winchester

with an APPENDIX and
Illustrations from old prints and pen and ink
drawings by
H. HODGSON, M.B., J.P., of Alresford
and URSULA OXLEY

Alresford:
LAURENCE OXLEY
The Studio Bookshop.

First published privately in 1937.
Revised edition 1969.
Second Impression 1970.
Third Impression 1973.
Fourth Impression 1978.
Sixth Impression 1986.

Printed and bound in Great Britain by
Antony Rowe Ltd, Chippenham

ISBN 0 950 1347 08

FOREWORD

The publishing of a Second Edition of this little history has seemed to me a very worth-while project in view of the fact that the original, printed in 1936, has been out of print for several years, and it is rarely that a copy passes through my hands.

The text has not been altered, but to replace plates not now available, I have introduced several new drawings by my wife, Ursula Oxley, of buildings in Alresford as they look today. The town retains much of its old-world charm, and this is borne out in these illustrations. There is also an original etching by Mr. A. E. Wade of the old Norman bridge at the bottom of Broad Street.

LAURENCE OXLEY,
The Studio Bookshop,
Broad Street,
Alresford,
Hampshire.

1969.

ILLUSTRATIONS

INTRODUCTION.

In 1774, Robert Boyes, Master of Perin's Grammar School, Alresford, drew up an MS. History of Alresford at the request of Sir Thomas Gatehouse, of Hedley Park, Co. Hants, who in his MS. " Survey of the County of Southampton " compiled in 1778 and dedicated to the Duke of Chandos has inserted an abridgement of Boyes' narrative.

Boyes revised his account in 1781 and prefixed to it an "Apology" explaining his reasons for its compilation.

This revised account—the original of 1774 annotated and corrected—is now in the Public Library of Winchester.

He must have had a suspicion that the results of his investigations would never see the light and that his notes would soon be neglected and forgotten, and so he apparently made a copy for circulation " amongst such as are anyway interested in the prosperity of the inhabitants or have any particular attachment to the place." He wrote in the "Apology " that he considered " that it could give no pleasure to anyone whilst lying in a heap of dusty papers, but circulated it might at least afford a short amusement to some." That was the main purpose of the literary entertainments of the age, the histories of particular cities and places, so he said, and " Why may not the good people of Alresford be gratified in the same way ? " "A treat from so obscure and confined a spot cannot but be plain and simple, and therefore insipid to epicures and connoisseurs, but this can be no reason why the plain-living inhabitants of Alresford may not be as well satisfied with the homely fare of their own native soil, as others of more refined taste may be with a splendid profusion of costly and delicate viands."

Some of those among whom the copy which he made was circulated seem to have found it so much to their taste that they in their turn made copies too, and these are continually turning up from time to time but without the author's name, with the consequence that speculation has been rife, and generally to a certain George Rodney of Old Alresford, a relation of Admiral Lord Rodney of naval fame, their origin has been attributed.   The Hampshire Field Club in 1925 published extracts from a history of Alresford by Sir George Brydges Rodney, which extracts in the exact words of Boyes show that his history, *circa* 1768—1782, was only one of the many copies.   From one of the manuscript copies Miss Mary Sandford, then living at North Court, Bishop's Sutton, made a typewritten copy which she presented to me for deposit in the safe of New Alresford Rectory.   Another copy has been lent to me by Miss Amy Hall, of Broad Street, Alresford ;   and yet another, the property of Mr. Willis, Curator of Basingstoke Museum, which in 1836 was possessed by a Mr. Thomas Skinner, who evidently added to it, recording events to date, has recently come into my hands. Either Mr. Skinner or someone else to whom it passed inserted newspaper cuttings as late as 1857.

This little manuscript book is the basis of the story which I now endeavour to present to a wider public and in a more durable form. It makes little attempt at sequence. I have tried to set things forth " in order."

Mine is in no sense a transcription of any of the copies I have seen ;   none the less it is the history of Alresford " according to " Robert Boyes, the author of 1774.   I give his facts and his opinions as he recorded them :   whether his facts are certain or his opinions sound I do not pretend to say.

I have preserved to a large extent the phraseology of the manuscripts and also the spelling, which is sometimes quaint.

An appendix is added bringing the history of Alresford down to the present day.

A. J. ROBERTSON.

Alresford.
   December, 1937.

ALRESFORD.

ALRESFORD takes its name from the river near it, which in the Saxon language may signify the Ford at the Alders, and as that part of the river which runs from Bishop's Sutton to Alresford Pond is in the Saxon Boundaries called the Woodford, it is possible that there may have been a number of alders growing somewhere near it. Camden calls the river by the name of Arle, but the ancient records of the Bishopric of Winchester describe it by no other name than the Itchen. The river rises from several springs on the East and North of Alresford Town, one of them at the upper part of Bishop's Sutton, one as far up as the middle of Ropley Dean, and another at Bighton. These meet together in Alresford Pond. Another rises in the upper end of Old Alresford Street and joins the others in Alresford Marsh near the Dean Bridge. Another stream (the Tichborne stream), rises at Bramdean and taking with it the springs of Hinton Ampner and Kilmeston, runs through Cheriton and Tichborne (where it forms a moat round Tichborne House) and falls into the Itchen in the West end of Alresford Marsh. Yet another stream rises at Candover, sometimes as far up as Preston Candover, and passing through Chilton and Brown Candover, Northington and Swarraton, forms a beautiful piece of water in the East of Northington Park at the Grange. Thence it takes its course to Abbotstone Lake, a fine seat of the Duke of Bolton (now taken down), and unites with the Itchen near a place called the Burrow where the several parishes of Alresford, Tichborne, Ovington, and Itchen meet together. From the Burrow it runs through the villages to Winchester and from thence into the sea near Southampton.

Hollingshead in his *Chronicle* published in 1586 calls the river as well below as above Winchester by the name of the Alresford. The Alresford, he says, " beginneth of divers fair springs about a mile from Alresford or Alford as it is now called," and he traces its course thus : " first with one bottom where it becomes a broad lake which for the most part is called Alresford Pond whence it goeth through a stone bridge at the end of Alresford Town. Thence leaving the Town on the left hand to Itchen Stoke. Below Itchen Stoke it cometh from Ovington by Easton Village and to Worthie. The great stream cometh from Worthie to the East Bridge (Winchester) and to S. Elizabeth college where it doth part in twain environing of the said house in a most delectable manner. After which it goeth to S. Cross leaving it a quarter of a mile on the right hand, then to Twyford a mile lower where it gathereth again into one bottom and goeth six miles further to Woodmill taking the Otter Brook withal on the East side and so into the salt creek that leadeth down to the ' Haven.' "

THE ' LIBERTY ' OF ALRESFORD.

THE Liberty of Alresford, comprehending the parishes of Old Alresford, New Alresford and Medstead, extends nearly nine miles in length from East to West, and is bounded Eastward by Bentworth, Alton, Chawton and Farringdon, on the South by Ropley, Bighton, Sutton and Tichborne, on the West by Tichborne, Ovington and Itchen Stoke, and on the North by Itchen Stoke, Abbotstone, Godsfield, Wield and Bentworth.

It belonged to the Bishops of Winchester upwards of 1000 years, having been given to the Church at Winchester by Kerniwalla, King of the West Saxons, about the middle of the seventh century. The earliest reference to Alresford in the Saxon records in the possession of the Dean and Chapter of Winchester is an edict of King Ena in 701. The above-cited grant of Alresford by King Kenwale was confirmed by King Edward about the year 826, by Edward the Elder in 908, by King Edwy in 956, and after that by King Edgar. Each of these edicts was subscribed by the particular King who granted it, and in several of them mention is made that this territory had in the reign of

King Alfred been seized upon and applied to secular use, but that it had been redeemed by Bishop Doniwulph and by him restored to the Church again. Alresford is described in most of them as consisting of forty farms or dwellings.

In *Doomsday Book*, a survey made by Commissioners appointed in almost every county in the kingdom by William the Conqueror in 1081 and finished in 1086, mention is made that in the time of Edward the Confessor it consisted of fifty-one hides of land. The intent of this Survey was to learn the value of the lands and thereby to discover what impositions the inhabitants could bear, that they might be taxed accordingly.

In this *Doomsday Book* we find only two principal tenants in the whole Liberty of Alresford—the Bishop or Chief Lord and under him Robert Dear, and one Englishman. The Bishop had in his domain 48 villains or villagers, 36 Borders or cottagers, and 31 slaves. The other had 27 villains, 6 Borders, and 19 slaves. So that upon the whole there were then 117 tenants of base tenure exclusive of the slaves.

Of the number of tenants in the Tythings of Old Alresford and Medstead we have no knowledge, but we can but suppose it to have been much less, for in the Survey taken long after in the reign of King Edward VI there were no more than 27 Copyholds within both these villages.

THE RECTORY OF ALRESFORD
(*i.e.* of Alresford ' Liberty ').

THE Rectory of Alresford, which also includes the several parishes of Old Alresford, New Alresford and Medstead, contains upwards of 6000 acres of arable meadow pasture and woodlands which for many years produced revenue to the Rector of about £500 a year, which has lately been improved to about £680 per annum, but out of this income the taxes, salaries of curates, etc., make a considerable deduction ; for the churches of New Alresford and Medstead being nearly six miles distant from each other, there have generally been two curates, one at each of these

GODFREY DE LUCY BRIDGE
ALRESFORD

JULY 1968 WWade

two places, who have handsome salaries* allowed them.
This living for several years past has generally been accompanied with some other ecclesiastical preferment and has several times since the Reformation been the option of the Metropolitan. The church of Old Alresford is the mother church, those of New Alresford and Medstead being only chapelries.

THE TOWN OF NEW ALRESFORD.

ALTHOUGH within the Liberty of Alresford, New Alresford was from the time of William the Conqueror until 1850 a chapelry of the Rectory of Alresford with Old Alresford as its mother church. It must have been recognised as a distinct parish before the days of the Norman Conquest and perhaps before the days of Edward the Confessor, as we find that there were then three churches within the Liberty of Alresford.

Concerning the rise of New Alresford there has been a tradition amongst the inhabitants which as it is remarkable it shall here be introduced and to the reader it must be left to judge what credit it deserves.

The story is that the Saxons, but at what time our tradition does not inform us, having engaged and totally defeated a body of the Danes in or near a village called Tistwood or Tisted about 5 miles east of Alresford, granted them quarter on condition of their going to the Ford of Arle to be baptized, with which the Danes complied. That in commemoration of this victory a sumptuous statue of the Virgin Mary was erected in the Churchyard of Old Alresford, and that great numbers of persons afterwards resorted from all parts to pay their devotions to the shrine. That these devotees became at length so numerous that the few houses standing within a convenient distance from it could not afford them proper accommodation, upon which account houses began to be erected upon the ground where New Alresford now stands. These increased to such an extent that New Alresford became in time a place

* See note in appendix p. 46 where the handsome salary is named.

of considerable trade and consequence. The truth of this story however is much to be questioned, though there are some circumstances which are strongly in favour of it.

There are still to be seen four huge burrows lying close together by the side of the Gosport turnpike road leading towards London, in a lane called Burrow Lane in the parish of West Tisted, from which it may be presumed that at some time or other there has been a considerable slaughter at or near this place, but whether it was the effect of a battle between the Saxons and the Danes or at what time it happened it is not at this time easy to discover.

There is also in the South-East part of Old Alresford Churchyard a mound or hillock which has generally been said to contain the ruins of an ancient place of devotion, and in a Survey of the Manor of Old Alresford taken in the reign of King Edward the Sixth, in describing the buildings and courtyards belonging to the Manor House, mention is made of an ancient chapel which had stood on or near this very spot. In 1769, whilst the tower was building, a farmer of the village had the curiosity to take one of the workmen with him, who with a pickaxe made a small opening into this mound when he discovered the foundations of a very strong wall and a kind of pavement within it, but did not proceed to make any further discovery.

But if there really was such an action at Tisted and attended with so remarkable a consequence, it is strange that the histories of those times should in general omit to mention it. They do tell us that in the first year of the reign of Ethelwulf the Danes landed at Southampton, but we do not find that they advanced so far up the country as Tisted or even to Alresford. The account they give us of an action between the Saxons and the Danes at Yaltendon in Hampshire in the reign of Alfred (anno 878), wherein he is said to have vanquished the Danes and obliged them to embrace Christianity and caused numbers of them to be baptized at Aller in Somersetshire instead of Arle in Hampshire, sounds very like the story concerning their defeat at Tisted and what is by tradition supposed to have been done at Alresford in consequence of it. Perhaps the near resemblance between the names Aller and Arle may have occasioned a misrepresentation of the matter.

ALRESFORD'S RISE TO BEING A PLACE OF IMPORTANCE.

WHILE the kings made Winchester their place of residence and the Parliaments were held there, Alresford must have been a place of great resort and thoroughfare on account of its nearness to that city, lying as it did on the direct road to London and other eastern parts of the kingdom.

Winchester, when the Saxon monarchy attained its highest grandeur, was the metropolis of the whole kingdom, and after the Norman Conquest continued to be a great and populous city for several ages, and there was not a single village or perhaps so much as a single house on the road between Alresford and the eastern suburbs of the city, consequently Alresford must have been a necessary place of rest and refreshment for many travellers. The many exclusive privileges of Charters of Exemption, which merchants and citizens of Winchester from time to time obtained by the favour of divers Princes, made their trade very great and extensive in many branches besides those of wool and leather for which it became the grand staple of the kingdom. The effect of this could not but be felt by the inhabitants of Alresford on account of their situation. In 1187 King Henry the Second confirmed their Charters of Privileges and Immunities, investing the chief magistrate of Winchester with the title of Mayor. In 1207 King John granted them a new and still more extensive Charter, wherein amongst other privileges he vested them with coinage and exchange of money for the whole kingdom, to be held and executed within the city of Winchester, and ordained that the citizens should be free to buy and sell in all fairs and markets toll free, and their goods and chattels to be discharged of all manner of tolls, bridge money, customs and duties throughout England and by all the seaports, etc., etc.

MAP OF HAMPSHIRE by PIETER VAN DEN KEERE 1599

In 1242 their Charters were still further enlarged by Henry the Third. In the reign of King Edward the First, A.D. 1302, a composition was made between the Corporation of London and the citizens and merchants of Winchester of certain disputes which had subsisted between them concerning their respective liberties and privileges, by which composition the Corporation of London confirmed their exemption from bridge-fare and wall-fare and from all duties for the shew or sale of cloth and all other customs usually levied for the sale of goods, wares and merchandise except the ancient tax upon wool, *viz.* sixpence on the first pack and fivepence a pack afterwards, and in 1353 King Edward the Third appointed Winchester the grand staple of the land for wool, woolfalls and leather.

Now in 1189 Godfrey de Lucy was consecrated Bishop of Winchester, who formed a noble and magnificent plan for improving the trade both of Winchester and Alresford by the establishment of a navigation on the River Arle or Itchen, which stupendous work he is said to have undertaken and completed at his own expense. In order to accomplish this vast undertaking he caused the great ware between Old and New Alresford to be thrown up where the springs between Alresford, Bighton and Sutton met together—which formed the head of that grand canal or reservoir called Alresford Pond—and by this means there has been ever since a sufficient head of water to keep the navigable river well supplied without danger of overflowing, and having brought the rivers and streams below into a regular channel, he furnished it with sluices, locks and aqueducts in proper places, to make it navigable for barges, lighters and other small vessels to trade from Alresford to Winchester and from thence to the sea near Southampton and so into all parts of the world.

In consequence of this great undertaking King John granted to the Bishop and his successors for ever the following Charter, A.D. 1214 :—

" John by the grace of God King of England, Duke of Normandy, etc., etc., to all Archbishops, Bishops, etc., and others our loving subjects sendeth greeting.

B

Know ye that by these presents we have granted unto our venerable Father Godfrey Bishop of Winchester and to all his successors for ever, free licence and authority to take receive collect and apply to his and their own proper use and advantage by himself or Bailiff, all fines tolls taxes and customs arising from the goods wares and merchandizes which shall or may hereafter be conveyed up or down the River Itchen, which the said Bishop hath now caused to be first trenched and made navigable at his own expense. Wherefore he shall receive on all goods wares and merchandizes the customs and tolls hereinafter specified (that is to say) For all dry Hides Falls and tanned skins 2d. etc."

It would be needless to particularize all the various kinds of goods specified in this Charter and which are said to have been usually carried up and down this river at its first institution : it may be sufficient to observe that the trade both of Winton and Alresford by means of the navigation must have been rendered infinitely more considerable and extensive.

The Bishop no doubt foreseeing this, and considering how necessary the latter would be to the advantageous carrying on the then vast trade and commerce of the former, and for the better supplying of its then numerous inhabitants, seems to have intended Alresford not only to be a kind of auxiliary mart, but also a wharf and magazine, as well for the goods, wares and merchandizes which were continually sending off from Winchester towards London and the eastern parts of the kingdom, as for the various kinds of goods and materials, fuel, corn and other provisions and necessaries of life which necessarily must be continually bringing in from the towns and villages adjacent to Alresford for the supply of that then great and populous city. He being in right of his Bishopric Lord of Alresford and the inhabitants being all his tenants.

This Bishop Godfrey de Lucy had the whole of the town of Alresford taken down and new modelled, and to render his plan the more commodious and magnificent

Centre of Alresford. Site of Old Market House

H. Hodgson

caused it to be laid out and new built in the form in which it now stands, *viz.* the streets broad, spacious and regular with a noble square in the centre for the Market Place.* He is said also to have given it the name of New Market, but the country people still retained its former name New Alresford to distinguish it from the sister village.

ALRESFORD AT
THE HEIGHT OF ITS PROSPERITY.

IF we may suppose that the Bishops in those times frequented and resided at their palace at Sutton which is not a mile from Alresford, and that Bishop Lucy in particular did so, it is very probable that many of the inhabitants were personally known to him ; they were all his tenants, and perhaps several of them tradesmen or workmen who served the Bishop or his household whilst at Sutton in the branches they were concerned in, and this might be a particular motive for his doing them a favour in the execution of a plan which he had formed, besides the propriety of it in the grand design of his new modelling the town. Perhaps at the same time he enfranchised their tenures and procured a Royal Charter for creating New Alresford a free borough and establishing a Corporation therein. If New Alresford was not a free borough in the time of Bishop Lucy, it certainly became so very soon afterwards. For it appears in the records in the Town of London that it sent representatives to parliament in the reign of Edward I, and in the Pipe Roll of the Bishopric for the tenth year of King John which is the most ancient Pipe now extant in the muniments at Wolvesey it is called the Borough of Alresford.

The Corporation of Alresford consisted of a bailiff or portreeve and eight burgesses, which are still kept up though they no longer send representatives to parliament. At what time the privilege of their enfranchisement ceased none of the inhabitants at present know, but the

* The Market House standing at one end of the Square and the great Corn Mills and Public Ovens and Boating House at the other end of it.

THE BELL HOTEL, WEST STREET

account they give of it is that as the representatives were
paid by their constituents for attendance in parliament
and the time came when they were either unable or un-
willing to bear that expense, they therefore prayed to be
disenfranchised, which they say Romsey, Basingstoke and
other Boroughs also did at the same time.   Nevertheless
this New Alresford still retains the name of a Borough,
and is as a Borough and Liberty of itself distinct from all
other hundreds and divisions in the County.   The bailiff
is every year elected by the majority of the burgesses for
the time being, in a Court which they annually hold for
that purpose in the month of August, at which Court they
also fill the vacancies of the burgesses.

ALRESFORD   POND.

THIS Pond when first made by Bishop Godfrey de Lucy
(as before described) was much larger than it is now.   It
is said to have extended over a mile in length, *viz.* from the
great ware on the West to a palace or mansion house of the
Bishops of Winchester then standing at Bishop's Sutton
on the East, and we are told that boats were wont to pass
up and down on this canal between the palace and the
town.

The Bishops of Winchester had formerly no less than
ten castles, palaces or manor houses accommodated for
the reception of themselves and their retinue, *viz.* Wolvesey,
Southwark,   Waltham,   Marwell,   Highclere,   Farnham,
Esher, Wargrave, Taunton and Sutton, to all of which
they resorted and lived according to the customs of the
times on the produce of their own estates.   Besides what
was produced on their demesne lands kept in their own
hands, their copyhold tenants were bound by their tenures
to bring in certain portions of wood, corn, poultry, eggs,
etc., for the supply of the Bishop's table and household.
There is great reason to suppose the Bishops frequently
resided at Sutton because there are larger wheat rents
paid to the Bishop by the copyhold tenants of Sutton than
from any other manor in the Bishopric, besides which they

were obliged to deliver in above 100 loads of wood and near 200 poultry every year. The walls of very large buildings are now to be seen at Sutton which are said to be the ruins of this palace, and doubtless it was so, for the spot where they stand is granted by lease from the Bishop under the description of the site of the Manor of Sutton. In those days the pond is supposed to have covered near 200 acres of land, but the mud and rushes through length of time and neglect have gradually encroached upon its borders. A great part of it has been converted into water meadows and much more remains overrun with sedges and rushes so that when the water is at its highest it does not now extend to above four score acres, and if neglected it will continue to diminish. It is stocked with immense quantities of fish, namely pike, trout, perch, carp, roach and eels, all of which will here grow to a very large size and are esteemed excellent in their several kinds. Pike have been caught in this pond between thirty and forty pounds weight, tench four or five pounds and perch two pounds each. Of eels there have been two and a half tons taken in one night and frequently above a ton about the months of September and October in dark, rainy nights. There formerly used to be a number of bream in the pond, but at present there are none to be found.

It is a fine piece of water and has usually had several boats kept upon it, and being stocked with a number of swans and other water-fowl it has a very pleasing appearance. When the weather is severe large flocks of wild fowl, chiefly ducks, widgeon and teal, and sometimes wild geese and ' hooping ' swans, etc., resort hither in the winter, especially in a time of hard frost, and some of them, *viz.* ducks, curwidgeon and coots, sometimes remain all the year and breed. Of coots there are at all times a great number, as also moorhens, water-rails and dabchicks or didappers. Divers other kinds of birds are also frequently seen here, *viz.* bitterns, herons, cormorants, sea-pies, gulls, curlews, red swallows, oxey-birds, sea-larks, kingfishers and sometimes cranes, and great number of snipe, lap-wings, plovers, which feed in the bordering meadows and pastures. In autumn an incredible number of starlings visit this pond every evening about sunset. Such immense flights of them are sometimes gathered together that they darken the spots over which they pass. They come in from all parts of the country for many miles round, and hover about in the air till the several flights are collected together, which keep coming for some hours in small companies and join the grand body, and at the close of the evening they drop all together into the sedge growing by the side of the pond, generally out of reach of gunshot, where they remain till the morning. As soon as the day begins to dawn a single bird gives the note of alarm and a general buzz instantly succeeds, and in a very short space of time they generally rise up together and presently detach themselves into small flights and go off into different parts of the country where they remain and feed in small parties till toward the next evening, and then they instantly return in like manner till about Christmas when they disappear and are no more seen till autumn in the next year. When the grand flight is hovering in the air which they always do till the several parties come in, they are frequently pursued by buzzards, kites and other rapacious birds, and on these occasions the various positions and evolutions they form themselves into in resisting or pursuing their enemy are very curious and entertaining, and the whole is astonishing to strangers to behold.

THE DECLINE OF ALRESFORD'S PROSPERITY.

In the reign of King Edward the Third, Winchester was the grand staple or settled market for the whole realm in the wool and leather trade, the staple having been removed thither from Brabant in 1352. Alresford prospered with it and commerce was 'immensely great.' But this did not last for long. The staple was removed from Winchester to Calais and Melcome Regis, putting an end to this commercial glory. Winchester and Alresford suffered together. In Winchester the streets and buildings where manufactures had been carried on were deserted, the houses tumbled down for the want of tenants, the churches ran to decay through disuse and neglect, the navigation failed, the river was suffered to break down the banks and forsake its regular channel, and that vast appearance of trade and commerce for which the city had become famous in the world vanished away and gave place to poverty and depopulation in so extreme a degree that within the space of eighty years after they had lost their trade and manufactures eleven considerable streets were run wholly to ruin and above 1000 houses with seventeen parish churches had fallen to the ground. As may appear by petition presented to King Henry VI in 1452 wherein these calamities are particularly represented. It must have been a very severe stroke on the trade and prosperity of Alresford, which depended in a great measure on that of Winchester and the navigable river.

But it was followed by a calamity still more shocking, for in the reign of Edward IV a pestilence so raged at Alresford that the place is said to have been almost wholly deserted and the inhabitants were reduced to so wretched a situation that even the Bishop's quit rent could not be collected. They seem however to have in some degree recovered themselves after these misfortunes and to have carried on a considerable trade or manufacture in the clothing way for many years after, for in the reign of Henry VIII there were several clothiers, dyers, etc., amongst the inhabitants and no less than four fulling mills standing within about a mile from the town. One fulling mill in Alresford Marsh, called Jennings or Black Mill, another in the same Marsh called New Mill, another near the borough called Willow or Far Mill, another Buddlesham Mill on Fobdown Water. There were also six corn mills very near the town, four of them inside one roof called the Town Mills, another at the Ware House called Ware Mill, and one other near Dean Bridge called Andrew's Mill, but even these branches gradually declined till at length their chief departure in trade seems to have been on the dealing and custom of their neighbours and friends in the adjacent villages.

There was no capital convenient in or near the town from which the tradesmen could reap any material benefit. The only foundation they had of the kind was a small society consisting only of a warden and five priests who had some land and tenements within the precincts of New Alresford.

They were of the Order of Jesus, and their chantry or oratory is said to have stood at the entrance into New Alresford churchyard and their house of residence, now the property of a tradesman near it, still passes in the Deeds of Conveyance of it by the name of Jesus House.

At the time of the Dissolution of the religious houses their lands and tenements were seized by King Henry VIII, and by letters patent of Queen Elizabeth dated April 4, 1589, they were granted to Richard Bramthwaite and Roger Bromley, Esquires, and their heirs for ever to be holden of the Queen and her successors as of the Manor of East Greenwich in Kent by fealty only in free and common soccage. They are since sold and dispersed into different hands.

THE TIME OF THE REFORMATION.

ABOUT the time of the Reformation the inhabitants of Alresford seem to have been again at a very low ebb, many of them having but little other dependance for support than what they could raise from the cultivation of a few acres of land they severally occupied within the Liberty of Alresford. The exercise of a trade and commerce was generally laid aside or but very feebly carried on amongst them and markets were deserted and universal poverty was taking place. In this deplorable state of affairs, the then Bishop of Winchester as lord of the Borough interested himself in the recovery of their prosperity, and with this view interfered in having the vacancies in their Corporation filled up of the most considerable persons among the inhabitants, and granted to the bailiff and burgesses certain liberties and franchises by Deed or Charter. The bene-volent exertions of the Bishop at the time they were reduced to so low and languid a state, and particularly this committing to the bailiff and burgesses the perpetual management and emoluments of the fairs and markets, proved a good foundation for the recovery of their trade and prosperity. But there were other accidental circumstances which also contributed to their advancement, particularly the unhappy troubles in the reign of Charles the First.

1644.

ON the 29th of March, 1644, a battle was fought at Cheriton Down, only two miles from Alresford, between the Royal Army under the command of Lord Hopton and the Parliamentary forces under Sir William Waller. The King's troops for a while seemed to have the better of it, but Col. Norton, who resided at the Manor House, Old Alresford, and who had used to hunt in this part of the country and was acquainted with all the roads and byeways, brought a fresh party of horse unexpectedly on the rear of them, by which manoeuvre they were soon defeated with considerable loss.

Whether or not in consequence of this help that came from Alresford or because of personal friendship with Colonel Norton, Oliver Cromwell frequently lodged at the Swan, Alresford, and finding several of the principal inhabitants warmly attached to his party it is said that not only did he recommend the tradesmen in general among his friends, but was himself particularly serviceable to several of the townsmen. Mr. Hildsley, at that time the owner of Alresford Farm, was afterwards made one of the Commissioners for vacant benefices.

Arthur Lipscombe, inn holder at New Alresford and also a proprietor of lands in Old and New Alresford, was appointed Bailiff and receiver of the rent of the several manors and estates within the Bailiwick of Sutton, and had two of his sons provided for in the Army. And Mr. Hancock, then a considerable tradesman in the town, is said to have received particular marks of Cromwell's favour.

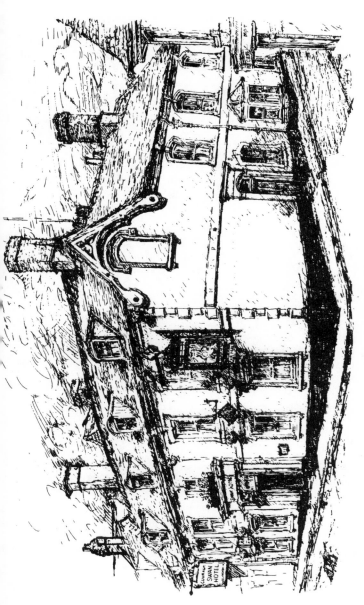

The Swan Hotel
(Oliver Cromwell often stayed here).

The gentry residing near the place coming thus to countenance and encourage its trade, a considerable business was carried on in the fleece and wool trade, and several opulent tradesmen made large returns in the shop and mercantile way. Several waggons were kept employed weekly in carrying wool bought up in Hampshire and Sussex for sale at Devizes and other clothing towns in Wilts, Somerset and Gloucestershire, and bringing back cheese and bacon and such other commodities as were the produce of those counties for sale at Alresford. Besides this much business was carried on in the malt trade, chandlery, tanning, sewing. Brewing and divers other branches and considerable contracts for Government were undertaken by some of the inhabitants.

FIRE.

ALL this revived prosperity received a most serious setback by reason of a great fire which occurred on the 1st day of May, 1689, when almost the whole town, together with the church and council house, was burnt to the ground. It was supposed to have been wantonly or maliciously set on fire, as it is said to have broken out in three different parts of the town at the same time. A party of soldiers who had marched out of the place just before it was discovered were suspected of being the authors of it, but this was never proved.

By this lamentable accident most of the inhabitants were deprived of a considerable part of their substance and became destitute of habitation and almost every convenience for carrying on their several trades and businesses.

The nobility and gentry in the County and elsewhere were very bountiful towards the relief of the sufferers, and a Royal Brief couched in very peculiar and pathetic terms excited compassion throughout the whole kingdom. In spite of all however their dividends upon the whole fell short of one-third part of their losses, so that several families sunk under the weight of their misfortunes and others laboured under great difficulties.

The following is an extract from the original brief which is here inserted on account of its being expressed in a way different from the common brief for fires :—

" William and Mary by the Grace of God King and Queen of England, Scotland, France and Ireland, to all and singular Archbishops, Bishops, Deans, etc., Greeting. Whereas we are credibly informed and given to understand by a certificate made at the general Quarter Sessions holden by adjournment at the Castle of Winchester in our county of Southampton on the 4th day of June in the first year of our reign under the hands and seals of our trusty and well-beloved Sir Charles Wyndham, Knight, Thomas Jervoise, Senior, Charles Morley, Edward Chute, Francis Dickins and Thomas Jervoise, Junior, Esqs., Justices of the peace for our said County, that on the 1st day of May last past there happened a sudden and most disastrous fire in the Borough of New Alresford in our said County, which through the boisterousness of the wind burnt so furiously that in the space of three hours the dwelling houses of above a hundred and seventeen families were destroyed with their warehouses, outhouses, barns and stables and great quantities of wares, goods, and household stuffs and also the Church, Chancel and Market House of the said Borough to the utter undoing of the inhabitants of the said place and the impoverishment of the country adjacent through the decay of trade, it being a great and very considerable market Town. The damage sustained thereby amounting to above Four and Twenty Thousand Pounds as appeared to our said Justices of the peace not only by the oaths of several of the inhabitants of the said Borough but also by the oaths of divers Carpenters, Bricklayers, Plumbers and Smiths who viewed and valued the same.

" So that the poor sufferers, who before this extraordinary accident were ready and willing to relieve the necessities of others, are by reason of this calamity become great objects of charity themselves and most of them must labour under lamentable and heavy pressures if not relieved by the charitable help of tender-hearted and well disposed Christians. They have therefore humbly besought us to commiserate their sad condition and to grant unto them our gracious letters patent etc. Unto which their request we have condescended and do in a peculiar manner recommend them to the pious and charitable thoughts and considerations of all our said loving subjects, not doubting that when their distressed condition shall be made known, they will be touched with a fellow feeling of their brethrens afflictions and bountifully contribute to their relief.

" Know ye therefore that of our royal favour and princely compassion we have given and granted and by these presents do give and grant unto the said poor sufferers, free Power Licence and Authority to ask gather receive etc. the alms and charitable contributions of all our loving subjects. Not only householders but servants strangers and others in all and every our Cities Towns Parishes etc. throughout England and Wales and the Town of Berwick upon Tweed towards their support and relief. Wherefore we command you and every of you that at such times as the bearer or bearers hereof shall come or repair to any of your churches chapels or congregations to ask and receive the alms, that you justly permit them so to do without any let or contradiction. And you the said Parsons Vicars and Curates upon some Lordsday within one month next after those our Letters Patent shall be produced or a true copy thereof tendered unto you or the Church or Chapel wardens respectively, shall deliberately and affectionately publish and declare the true tenor of the same unto our said loving subjects and earnestly exhort persuade and stir them up to extend their liberal contributions towards repairing their said losses and not to look on it as an ordinary Brief And for the further and more effectual collecting thereof, you the said Church-wardens, Chapel Wardens and Collectors for the Poor and their Overseers respectively are to go from house to

c

house upon the week days next following after the publication of these presents, to collect the alms etc. and to endorse the sums collected in words at length and not in figures on the copy of these presents and enter the same in your books of accounts for your several Parishes Chapels etc. where such respective sums were gathered, and to deliver the monies so gathered to the bearer or bearers hereof authorized herein together with such copies And we do appoint our trusty and well-beloved cousin, Charles Duke of Bolton, our right trusty and well-beloved Charles, Marquis of Winchester, the Right Reverend Fathers in God the Lord Bishops of London and the Lord Bishop of Winchester, Sir Nicholas Stuart, Baronet, Sir Hugh Stewkley, Baronet and Sir Charles Wyndham, Knight, Sir Robert Henley, Knight, Colonel Richard Norton, Doctor Nicholas, Warden of Winton College, William Harrison and Henry Hawkins Doctors in Divinity, James Venables, George Bridges and Henry Dawly Esquiers, Henry Perin M.D., and William Needham B.D. trustees and receivers for the said poor sufferers etc."

NOTE.

An original copy of this Brief is in the possession of the Town Trustees of Alresford. It concludes thus :—

"And lastly, Our Will and Pleasure is, that no Person or Persons whatever, shall Collect or Receive the said money of or from the Church-Wardens, Chappel-Wardens, Collectors for the Poor, and their Overseers, but such only as shall be appointed and authorized so to do, by Deputation under the Hands and Seals of the above named Receivers and Trustees or any five or more of them : Any Law, Statute, Act, Ordinance or Provision, heretofore made to the contrary hereof, in any wise notwithstanding. In Witness whereof, We have caused these Our Letters to be made Patents, and to continue for One Year from Michael-mas next ensuing the Date hereof, and no longer. Witness Ourselves at Westminster the Two and Twentieth Day of June, in the First Year of our Reign.

God save the King and Queen.

In the Savoy. Printed by Edward Jones for William Fall dwelling in Weld Street 1689."

Most of the dwelling houses and private buildings as well as the Church and Market House were in a short time rebuilt in a plain but decent manner and business in general was pursued.

The Bishop of Winchester furnished them with Trustees to build their church and the Marquis of Winchester and Colonel Norton also gave them the timber of their new Market House, which perhaps gave occasion to some writers to assert that the neighbouring gentry gave the sufferers all the timber for rebuilding their houses, which is unreasonable to suppose and indeed not true.

A general spirit of industry prevailed amongst them so that they whose circumstances would not admit of their supporting themselves and their families in the way they had done before this calamity befell them, betook themselves to some other employment and in general kept themselves from being burthensome to their already distressed neighbours, and (strange as it is to relate) within fifteen years after this lamentable event there was but one single person who received weekly alms of the parish. And for the space of forty-five years after there never were in any one year above four or five persons at the most on the weekly book at the same time.

During all which time the whole expense of the poor did not amount to above £35 per annum one year with another.*

The trade of the inhabitants has been all along increasing in almost every branch except the wool trade, which is now diverted into another channel. And although the number of the houses in Alresford Town does not exceed one hundred and seventy, yet it is said to pay a larger sum every year for duty to the King than the whole city of Winchester confined to its walls.

* In the year 1709 the whole sum disbursed by the Overseers amounted to £17. 12s. 9u., of which some £2. 12s. 6d., was given to 325 persons brought out of France who passed through Alresford.

PERIN'S GRAMMAR SCHOOL.

To the Henry Perin, M.D., appointed by the above Brief as Trustee for the sufferers in the great fire of 1689, Alresford owes the foundation of a free grammar school which for years was a benefit to the whole neighbourhood. It was founded in 1698 by Christopher Perin, Esq., then of Ware House in the Parish of Old Alresford, pursuant to the Will of his brother, Henry Perin, lately deceased. It was for the educating nineteen poor men's sons in Latin tongue, writing, accounts, etc. Six of these were to be the poor tradesmen's sons of New Alresford, five poor men's sons of the Parish of Old Alresford, four more poor men's sons of the Parish of Bishop's Sutton, and four more poor men's sons of the Parish of Cheriton. None were to be admitted scholars on the foundation till they were nine years of age or till they were brought to their schoolmaster to be examined by him and found qualified to learn the Latin grammar, and two sons of the same person were not to be on the foundation at the same time. Every scholar was to pay one shilling for his admission and one shilling a year towards providing rods and brooms to be used in the school. The government of the Charity was vested in eight Trustees and two Visitors. The Trustees were chosen of the neighbouring gentlemen, and whenever four of them were dead the survivors by the Will of the Founder were to appoint eight other gentlemen to succeed them and to convey the estate and trust to such eight new Trustees.

The schoolmaster and also the scholars were from time to time to be elected by a majority of the Trustees for the time being. The Rectors of Alresford, Cheriton, Bighton and Bishop's Sutton for the time being were perpetual Visitors and Governors of the School.

The schoolmaster (by the Will and decree above mentioned) might be a clergyman, but could not hold the school with any ecclesiastical benefice having cure of souls. And by the same authority he was left at liberty either to take in or refuse other scholars besides those on the

34 AND 36 WEST STREET, ALRESFORD

Foundation as he should think proper, so as the boys on the Foundation were not neglected.

The Founder furnished the school with a library for the use of the Master and scholars, and endowed it with about fifty acres of land in New Alresford, chiefly enclosed and lying all together except two or three small pieces in the Common Fields and one acre in the Marsh, the rents of which lands were (by the same Will and decree) directed to be received half-yearly by the schoolmaster for the time being for ever, except forty shillings a year which was to be paid to the Trustees and applied yearly as occasion might require in the repair of the buildings. Besides which the Founder charged certain copyhold estates lying within and held by the Manor of Bishop's Sutton with an annuity or rent-charge of five pounds a year to be received by the schoolmaster in like manner.

The School House is a plain, strong building standing at the bottom of the North side of the West Street and forming the angle of that and another called the Dean. The school is a large and very lofty room adjoining to the East end of the dwelling house. The offices stand on the North side of the school's School House forming two wings, one at the East end and the other at the West end, having a square court between them bounded by a pleasant rural garden on the North.

N.B.—For the subsequent history of this school see note in the Appendix (p. 37).

ANOTHER DEVASTATING FIRE.

ON the thirtieth day of April, 1736, fire broke out in a public brewhouse on the North side of the West Street in New Alresford which burnt down the greatest part of the street before it could be got under. For although it happened in the day time and great help was ready at hand, yet the wind blowing briskly from the north-west it carried the flames across the street to a great distance, and several of the outbuildings being covered with thatch they were almost instantly in flames, so that several of the sufferers had not time to save any considerable part of their goods and were in a very distressful situation. But they had a speedy consolation from the humanity and kindness of their neighbours and the bounty of several worthy personages. The Bishop of Winchester, the Duke of Bedford and Pawlet St. John, Esq., sent £50 apiece for their immediate relief, George Bridges, Esq., 40 guineas, John Barnard, Esq., £40. The Earls of Pembroke and De la Warr £25 each. The Duke of Chandos and Lord Lymington 20 guineas each. The Hon. John Spencer and Mr. Vernon £23 each, and besides these many liberal benefactions were speedily received from divers of the neighbouring clergy and gentlemen. In the city of Winchester above £130 was gathered, and most of the adjacent towns and villages made handsome collections, but still the loss of the sufferers was far from being repaired. They were therefore, after a considerable time, advised to apply for a Brief, which they obtained. But it had been so long deferred that it did not amount to so much as might have been expected if they had applied in that way immediately after the misfortune happened.

The cause of this delay was that the sufferers had been informed that the expenses of a Brief would be so great that there would be but little coming to them by it. Their Rectors, Mr. Soley and (after his death) Mr. Hoadley, were indefatigable in their endeavours to serve them, and through their hands they received benefactions to the amount of above five hundred pounds and about fourteen hundred pounds by their Brief. Upon the whole, after all expenses were deducted, the sufferers received about twelve shillings in the pound on their several losses.

The houses and buildings in general were soon after rebuilt much in the same state as they had been before the fire in a plain, decent manner with brick and covered with tiles, the sufferers coming to a general resolution to avoid thatch coverings in their new erections.

The following is an abstract of the Brief :—

" George the Second by the grace of God King of
Great Britain &c. To all Archbishops, Bishops etc.
greeting.

" Whereas it hath been represented unto us as well
upon the humble petition of Saul Newlyn, John
Meacher, William Collyer, William Westerton, John
Atkinson, Thomas Newell and John Murrant and
thirty other persons Inhabitants and sufferers by Fire
at the Town of New Alresford in the County of Southampton as by certificate under the hands and seals of
our trusty and wellbeloved The Hon. Edward Stowell
and George Bridges Esq., The Reverend Benjamin
Woodroffe, Edward Hooker and James Perkins Esqs.
and others our Justices of the Peace etc. made at their
general Quarter Sessions of the Peace held at the Castle
of Winchester etc. Anno 1740, that on the thirtieth
day of April 1736 a sudden and dreadful fire broke out
in the Brew house of the said Thomas Newell a Common Brewer, situate about the middle of the North
side of one of the high streets of the said Town which
by reason of the dryness of the season, and the wind
blowing directly across the said street communicated
the flames to both sides of the said street at once, and
thereby rendered all means to stop its progress in-
effectual ; so that in a space of about five hours it
burnt down and consumed not only the said Brew
house and Buildings with the stocks of Malt, Hops,
Beer, utensils and materials thereto belonging but also
all the dwelling houses, Malthouses, Warehouses,
Barns, Stables, outhouses and other buildings of above
seventeen of the inhabitants of the said Town together
with their household goods, wares, merchandizes,
stocks in trade, stocks of Corn and Hay, Beans, Malt,
Hops and large quantities of Beer in vaults and cellars,
working Tools and Implements in Trade and
Husbandry and likewise burnt and did great damage
to the Dwelling Houses and goods, wares and other
merchandizes of above thirty other inhabitants of the

said Town, besides those whose circumstances have not rendered them objects of charity, to the great danger of lives of the said sufferers and their families and to their exceeding great loss and impoverishment etc. The truth of the premises hath been made appear to our said Justices sitting in their open Court not only by and upon the oaths of the said poor sufferers but of several able and experienced workmen and others who were neighbours and eye witnesses to this grievous calamity and knew the circumstances of the said sufferers and made an estimate of the damages which on a moderate computation amounts to the sum of £3477 and upwards exclusive of Insurances etc."

The Trustees for the sufferers were the Dukes of Bedford, Beaufort and Bolton, the Bishop of Winchester, Lord Lymington, Lord Craven, Norton Pawlett, Anthony Henley, Thos. Bates, Henry Collins and William Yalden, Esquires, the Rev. John Hoadley, Richard Furney and William Sealey, Clerks, and Mr. William Hawkins, Robt. Coopp and Hilbourn Withy, gentlemen.

SMALL - POX.

ABOUT the year 1737 the small-pox having been likely to spread in the town, a house divided into three apartments was built in the West end of the piece of land called the Town Acre intended for the reception of such of the inhabitants as should sicken with that distemper, and there could not have been a more proper situation for the purpose. The expense of the building was raised by subscription, towards which Mr. Hoadley and Mr. Barnard gave £20 each and most of the substantial tradesmen and inhabitants subscribed from one to five guineas and almost all the householders, even the very labouring men, readily contributed what they could afford towards it. This erection has proved very beneficial to the inhabitants : for the small-pox has never spread in the town since that time. And at times when it had been rife at Winchester or other neighbouring market towns it has been the occasion of considerable advantage to the tradesmen and shopkeepers of Alresford by bringing many country people to their shops and markets who at other times dealt in other places.

LATER NOTE.

The house called the Pest House was taken down and the materials sold by consent of the parishioners at the time of the enclosure of the Common Fields in New Alresford, award dated 30th June, 1807.

NONCONFORMITY IN ALRESFORD.

ON the South side of the West Street near a house called St. Joans belonging to James Butler, Esq., there lately stood a meeting house for Quakers, but the sect having wholly failed in this neighbourhood it hath lately been taken down and is now thrown into Mr. Butler's gardens ; and it is remarkable that for above thirty years last past there has not been a single inhabitant of the town of any dissenting profession in religion, but all of them are and have been followers of the Established Church except three or four small families of Roman Catholics.

CHARITIES.

THERE are some few charitable establishments in favour of the Poor of New Alresford, but they are not very considerable. William Pink, who had himself been a poor vagrant and had received frequent kindnesses from many of the inhabitants of this town, at his death about the year 1670 left twenty pounds to the Parish Officers of New Alresford, the interest of which he directed to be paid yearly for ever to the poor of the town on S. Thomas' Day.

James Withers, a considerable tradesman of the town, by his Will in 1680 bequeathed twenty pounds to the Bailiff of the Borough, directing the interest thereof yearly for ever to be distributed by the Bailiff for the time being amongst poor widows and widowers · of the town on S. Thomas' Day.

One of the above-mentioned sums was laid out in the purchase of a house in the Dean, now used as a poor house, and one acre of land in the Common Fields now called the Town Acre, on part of which now stands the Pest House.

The other £20 was laid out in the purchase of four acres of land in the Marsh, for each of which twenty shillings a year is distributed amongst the poor.

William Todd of New Alresford, Gent., by his Will in 1681 left an annuity or rent-charge of three pounds a year to be distributed every year on Good Friday in the church porch of New Alresford, immediately after Morning Prayer, amongst such of the inhabitants as did not receive weekly alms of the town.

He charges five acres of land in Brook Furlong and two acres of land in the Marsh with the payment thereof for ever, which sum is constantly distributed amongst the poor every year on Good Friday by the Overseers as the Will directs.

LATER NOTE.

Jenny Harris, relict of William Harris, Esq., of this town, left by her Will (who died May 28, 1833) an annuity in trust of ten pounds a year to be distributed for ever on New Year's Day in bread or other provisions by the Churchwardens and Overseers.

In addition to the above :—

> In 1853 William Wilkinson,
> in 1862 John Dunn,
> in 1882 Christopher Cooke
> and in 1885 Susanna Eliza Covey

left sums of money for the benefit of the poor of the parish.

For the present system of administering the Charities see Appendix (p. 37).

APPENDIX.

PERIN'S GRAMMAR SCHOOL.

HENRY PERIN'S ideals and endowments having become at the end of the 19th century quite insufficient to meet the requirements of modern education and more particularly for those who were worthy of more than elementary instruction, the Charity Commissioners in 1899 formulated a scheme whereby co-education was introduced and training on modern lines was established. In 1909 the Charity Commissioners' scheme was repealed and a new scheme was made by the Board of Education whereby the school carried on in new premises provided by and vested in the Local Education Authority, *i.e.* the County Council, became a Public Secondary School for boys and girls.

In 1923 yet another scheme made by the Board of Education altered things once more ; the administration of the Foundation and its endowment was placed entirely in the hands of the County Council.

In 1932 the County Council closed the school as not fulfilling the purpose of a secondary school and because of the great expense which the education of the comparatively few children attending it entailed.

In 1934 the school was re-opened by the County Council as a Senior Elementary School educating children over 11 years of age from Alresford and the surrounding villages.

PRESENT SYSTEM OF ADMINISTERING THE ALRESFORD CHARITIES.

THE Board of Charity Commissioners for England on the 2nd of October, 1923, approved and established a scheme for the regulation of eight old Charities belonging to the Parish of Alresford of which the gross yearly income is £50. 16s. 0d.

The Body of Trustees appointed consists of five persons :—
    One ex-officio Trustee and
    Four Representative Trustees.

The ex-officio Trustee is the Rector for the time being of New Alresford, and the Representative Trustees are two appointed by the Parish Council and two appointed by the New Alresford Town Trust.

The manner in which the Trust is to be administered is very clearly defined and the Trustees have no power to depart from it. The yearly income is to be applied by the Trustees in making payments under one or more of certain specified heads : " for the benefit either of the poor of the Parish of New Alresford generally, or of such poor persons resident therein as are not in receipt of Poor-law relief other than medical relief, and in such a way as they consider most advantageous to the recipients and most conduces to the formation of provident habits."

Before however any such payments are made, it is laid down that the following curious periodical payment should be provided for in accordance with the Will of the testator : In every year in which the 26th day of June falls on a Sunday, out of the income of the Charity of Christopher Cooke the sum of £1 shall be paid to the Minister who shall deliver a sermon on that day from one of the Ten Commandments or a text in the Parish of New Alresford.

FRENCH PRISONERS.

As recorded in a footnote in the foregoing history, 323 prisoners brought out of France passed through Alresford in 1709 and received relief from the overseers.

In the several wars with France and Spain during the reign of King George the Second, Alresford was one of the places appointed for the residence of the Spanish and French prisoners of war on parole, and about the year 1757 the number of them at this place amounted to upwards of 300.

From 1808 to the year 1814 there were upwards of 200 French prisoners on parole at Alresford. Several of them died in Alresford and they were buried in the Churchyard, where their graves are still marked and cared for.

The French Prisoners' Graves in Alresford Churchyard

RECTORS OF NEW ALRESFORD.

FROM 1225 until 1850 the Liberty of Alresford consisted of the three parishes of Old Alresford, New Alresford and Medstead. The Church of S. Mary the Virgin, Old Alresford, was the Mother Church and New Alresford and Medstead were Chapelries. In 1850 the Parishes were divided.

The Rectors of New Alresford since the division have been :—

1851.	William Brodie.
1868.	William Sealey.
1879.	William Orde Newnham.
1889.	Alexander Arthur Headley.
1915.	Frederick George Gilbert Jellicoe.
1922.	Walter Edmund Colchester.
1925.	Andrew John Robertson,
	Hon. Canon of Winchester.

NEW ALRESFORD PARISH CHURCH.

THE following is from a short account published by the Rev. A. A. Headley, Rector (1889—1915), during whose incumbency the church was restored in 1898.

Godfrey de Lucy turned the little Norman church into an Early English one, probably more suited to the growing importance of the place. Portions of the walls of the church go back to his time and are perhaps even earlier. In the restoration of 1898 an Early English window was discovered and opened up, which Sir Arthur Blomfield considered to date from A.D. 1200. There is also a fragment of a column of the same date used in the new window of the chancel aisle. Whatever de Lucy's church may have been like, it made way about 1400 for one in the Perpendicular style. "About 1400 Alresford appears to have been consumed by fire " (*Sketches of Hampshire*, by Duthy, p. 104). The lower part of the present tower is probably earlier. The upper storey of brick may have been added

D

after the fire. This 1400 church must have been a beautiful building, consisting of nave, two aisles, a small side chapel south of the chancel, and the western tower. This stately church was in its turn burnt down in 1689. All that escaped was the tower and the outer walls of the nave. The people did the best they could by strengthening the outer walls, partly filling up the wide windows, using oak and chestnut trees for pillars, casing them in with painted deal and covering the whole with a heavily timbered " Hampshire Barn " roof. Outside, the roof was in three gables, as probably had been the roof of the Perpendicular church ; while inside there was a slightly domed white-washed ceiling reaching from the north wall to the south. The chancel was small and low, with three round-headed single-light windows, north, east, and south. There was also a western gallery. This church was re-opened in 1694 and the date inscribed on a stone over the east window of the chancel. Later on the outside of the church was covered with roughcast to keep out the damp, and the dates when this was done were inscribed on each wall. These dates misled the authors of Woodward and Willis' *Hampshire* to state : " The tower is of 1690, the south aisle 1760, the north aisle 1766, and the chancel 1767."

Further galleries were added about 1830 with dormer windows in the roof to give them light. The north chancel aisle was added later, and a vestry built south of the chancel in 1857. This did away with the windows in the north and south walls of the chancel. The east window was removed in 1879, when a three-light Early English window was inserted in memory of Mr. and Mrs. Marx. This window was moved into the chancel aisle in 1897, as well as a reredos given in 1883 in memory of Captain Marx. Previous to the restoration the chancel aisle was used as an organ chamber.

The roof and pillars gradually became decayed, till at last nothing could be done but remove all the work of 1644 and build a new church, utilizing the old walls and tower. Sir A. Blomfield was the architect, and from his

NEW ALRESFORD, HANTS, S.W.

OLD ALRESFORD, HANTS, N.

From the *Gentleman's Magazine*, 1811

Alresford Church, c. 1850

From an old Print

designs a handsome Perpendicular church was built, in which was carefully incorporated whatever was ancient, so that the story of the church as told by itself can be read more clearly now than was possible before the restoration. In throwing the chancel wall back some ten feet we came on the foundations of the earlier wall, so that the chancel is now the same length as the one which was burnt down, but is rather wider.

Many stone fragments were found, and the best specimens are preserved in the church. Among them are pieces of the Norman font, carved heads (probably corbels), portions of columns and windows, and a piece of a Tudor font. On the outer face of the tower is a small crucifix, the history of which is uncertain. It is undoubtedly of a great age. The church as restored has nave, aisles, chancel, chancel aisle and organ chamber, with vestry beyond. The nave is separated from the aisles by stone columns, over which is a clerestory, the roof above being of solid English oak. On the inside face of the tower may be seen the " housing course " of the old Perpendicular nave roof. The easternmost window of the south aisle is filled in partly with actual carved stones found in the restoration and partly with other old stones following their lines, so that it is probably an actual reproduction of the window which stood there in 1400 (circa).

The reredos in opus sectile work, representing the Last Supper, and the east window, with, in the central figure, " The glorified Christ," were designed and executed by Messrs. James Powell & Sons, of Whitefriars. These were given by Mr. H. H. Walford of Arle Bury, without whose generous aid the whole work of restoration would have been quite impossible. The bells were re-hung as a memorial in the Diamond Jubilee year, and a large addition to the churchyard was consecrated in 1900. The registers date from 1678 ; the earlier ones no doubt perished in the fire. Fortunately the Communion plate was saved, the chalice being Elizabethan.

CHURCH PLATE.

In the catalogue of the loan exhibition of plate at the Bournemouth Church Congress of 1935, the two most noteworthy pieces of plate in the possession of New Alresford Church were described as follows :—

" 1.   Chalice.   Silver.   The bowl is rather acutely tapered and has a moulded wire under the lip.   A band of the strap and foliated work found on Elizabethan chalices is engraved on it :   but this appears to be of comparatively recent date.   The stem has stamped nurl bands above and below with a flattened knop, the foot is slightly domed.   Marks :   London assay for 1564 and a fleur-de-lis for the maker.

" 2.   Paten.   Silver.   Plain with moulded wire edge and a high plain foot.   Marks :   London assay for 1695 and monogram A.N. for Antony Nelme, the maker. Inscription :   ' Deo Servatori Sacrum ' and at back ' Ex dono Rev. Viri Mri Hopkins Rectoris de Bighten.   A.D. 1695.   Sum capellae de Alresford Nova.' "

THE TOWER.

The tower consists of three stages.   The lowest is probably 15th century work, with a fine arch into the nave.   This arch escaped the fire, but the pillars supporting it suffered and were so mutilated, partly it may be in erecting the west gallery, that in 1898 they were much repaired.   Previous to 1857 the fire engine was kept in the tower.   In 1857 a flight of stairs was placed in the tower as the means of access to the galleries, which before that had been reached by staircases inside the church.   These were then done away with.   The galleries were removed altogether in 1898.

CRUCIFIX.

In the west face of the tower is a crucifix and in the north face a cross, not a defaced crucifix.   Sir A. Blomfield, who was the architect of the restoration of the church in 1898, considered these to be insertions, and that they had formed part of a churchyard cross.

In an article on " Pre-Conquest Architecture in the Parish Churches of Hampshire " in the *Winchester Diocesan Chronicle* of April 1913 the writer, Colonel H. L. Jessep, states : " In addition to the instances already mentioned of Anglo-Saxon sculpture, the following completes the list of all that is known to be in Hampshire :

" The rood, possibly of the 10th century, set into the reredos of the S.E. Chapel of Romsey Abbey, and a small stone crucifix built into the wall of the tower of New Alresford Church."

THE CHURCH BELLS.

Previous to 1811 there were six bells. In 1811 they were re-hung by Messrs. Mears & Stainbank and two were added, making a peal of eight.

In 1897 they were quarter turned, as the Diamond Jubilee Memorial.

In 1936 they were again turned, one bell which was cracked was recast and they were hung in a new iron frame. The cost of this together with necessary repairs to the Tower was £500. This was raised by subscription. The work was done by Messrs. John Taylor & Sons of Loughborough, and a tablet was placed in the Church Tower commemorating the restoration of the bells and the Silver Jubilee of King George V.

The inscriptions on the bells are as follows :— (1811).

TREBLE.	In sweetest sounds let each its note reveal Mine shall be first to lead the dulcet peal.
SECOND.	The public raised us with a liberal hand We come with harmony to cheer the land.
THIRD.	When female virtue weds with manly worth We catch the rapture and we spread it forth.
FOURTH.	Does battle rage, do sanguine hosts contend We hail the victor if he's Britain's friend.
FIFTH.	May he who England's matchless sceptre sways Her sacred honour guard, her glory raise.
SIXTH.	May Britons still their ancient freedom boast And flattering commerce bless their happy coast.
TENOR.	May all who I shall summon to the grave The blessing of a well spent life receive.

William Keene, James Redin are Churchwardens.

T Mears of London fecit 1811.

Alresford Church, 1937

All bear the maker's name, but the seventh no other inscription.

Peal Boards in the belfry record peals of Grandsire Triples rung on December 26, 1824, and December 31, 1837, by local men conducted by Mr. J. Harvey. Also a peal of Kent Treble Bob Major by members of the Winchester Guild after the bells were re-hung on December 22, 1897. Members of the Guild also rang a peal of Stedman Triples on January 26, 1907.

A peal of Triples was rung when the bells were opened after being augmented from six to eight on March 25, 1911, by ringers from various parts of the country.

On December 26, 1936, to commemorate the restoration of the bells the Winchester and Portsmouth Guild of Ringers rang a peal of Bob Major, 5,040 changes, in 3 hours 19 minutes. Apparently this peal is the only peal of Bob Major rung on the bells, and the two peals of Grandsire Triples in 1824 and 1837 the only peals by local men.

THE ORGAN.

The organ originally given in 1832 was a single manual. In Mr. Sealey's time (1868—1879) the Bourdon was added. In 1898 it was rebuilt and turned into a two-manual. In 1926 this organ was entirely rebuilt and considerably added to at a cost of £800.

It was opened and dedicated on May 10 by the Rev. E. C. Peake, Rector of Hinton Ampner and Rural Dean, when a Recital was given by Dr. A. Eaglefield Hull of Huddersfield.

PLURALITIES IN THE 18TH CENTURY AND THE STIPENDS OF ASSISTANT CURATES.

EXTRACTS FROM NEW ALRESFORD CHURCH REGISTERS, 1776—1777.

The Rev. J. Hoadly, LL.D., Rector of Old Alresford with the chapels of New Alresford and Medstead, Rector of S. Mary's near Southampton, Chancellor of the Diocese of Winchester, Rector of Overton (*sine cura*) and Master of S. Cross, died March 16th, 1776 at his parsonage house S. Mary's, Southampton.

The Rev. W. Buller, M.A., Prebendary of Winton, Canon of Windsor, Rector of Wonston and of Houghton, Hants, succeeded Dr. Hoadly in the Rectory of Alresford and in the Rectory of Overton (*sine cura*).

1782.

Curacies of Old and New Alresford consolidated.

Mem. November 4, 1782. The Rev. William Buller, D.D., the Rector and myself changed our agreement. The Curate was wont to receive £50 per annum for serving New Alresford, exclusive of surplice fees and Easter offerings, and to receive 10s. 6d. for serving Old Alresford each Sunday during the Rector's absence exclusive of surplice fees and Easter offerings. But now the Curate is to receive £73. 10s. per annum and to take upon himself the whole duty of both churches ; the sacrament-days at New Alresford excepted when the Rector is to be responsible for the duty at Old Alresford. The Easter offerings and surplice fees of both parishes belong to the Curate as usual.

The Rector ordered the new agreement to commence on the 29th of September 1782.

WILLIAM MASTERS, M.A., Curate.

By the above agreement the curacy is improved to the value of about six pounds.

William Masters, Curate for 21 years.   1797.

1804.

The full benefit of an act of the legislature (commonly called Buller's Bill) by which the Bishops were enabled under certain circumstances to grant to curates £75 salary and £15 for a house is extended to this cure !

The stipend is now £90 per annum and with the addition of fees and offerings in both parishes which (by agreement with the Rector) belong to the curate and which usually amount to about £25 the consolidated curacies of Old and New Alresford may be fairly averaged at £115 per annum.

GEORGE SHERER, Curate.

1836.

The organ erected in New Alresford Church, the gift of the Bailiff and Burgesses at a cost of nearly £150, was opened on Sunday, June 12th, 1836.

(MSS.)

OCTOBER 24, 1857.

Alresford. The interior of our Parish Church having undergone a thorough repair was opened on Sunday last for Divine worship. The old and inconvenient high seats have been replaced by very substantial pews. A large number of free sittings have been appropriated to the poor and a greater amount of accommodation has been secured to the parishioners ; the whole having been accomplished by voluntary contributions, aided by grants from the Incorporated Church Building Societies and through the untiring exertions of the Rector, the Rev. W. Brodie. . . . The pulpit, reading desk, and clerk's lectern are of carved oak, and of a very chaste design. The Altar cloth of Utrecht velvet, the beautiful carved table, faldstools, and tesselated pavement within the Altar rails were provided from a separate subscription, amounting to about £50, collected by the Sunday School teachers from the ladies of the town and neighbourhood. The work has been judiciously carried out under the superintendence of Mr. W. Hunt, the architect ; and the work executed by the tradesmen of the town, who have given general satisfaction. The Lord Bishop of the Diocese preached twice on the occasion and the sermons were impressive and appropriate, and liberal collections were made at the doors in aid of the Improvement Fund.

(Newspaper cutting.)

1859.

The Churchyard was enlarged by the addition of half an acre in the year 1859 at the cost of £180. **MSS.**

1862.

The Nave of the Church was built (? enlarged) by subscription for the increase of sittings in the year 1862 at a cost of £300. **MSS.**

OLD ALRESFORD.
(From the MS.)

THE Church of Old Alresford is the Mother Church, those of New Alresford and Medstead being only Chapelries annexed. This church has within a few years past been wholly taken down and rebuilt by the parishioners assisted by large allowances from the late and present Bishops of Winchester and liberal subscriptions from the Proprietors of Estates in the Parish. The body of the Church and the Chancel were taken down and rebuilt in 1753, the Tower in 1769, and the bells cast and hung in 1770. The old Church had only four bells, on one of which was the following motto :—[1]

SUM ROSA: PULSATA: MUNDI: MARIA: VOCATA.

---

[1] Duthy calls the Bell inscription " a barbarous and not very intelligible remnant of the superstition of days of yore ", and adds : It is hardly safe to indulge in any conjecture that might be hazarded as to the real age of this inscription from the form of its characters, for it is uncertain whether the letters have been faithfully and accurately delineated in the MS. from which they are here copied.

He suggests the middle word to be puncta or punctata, furnished with prickles as applied to the Rose. It has been otherwise rendered :—

Sum Rosa pulsata mundi Maria Vocata.

(MS. note left by Rev. A. A. HEADLEY, 1897).

and on another of them was a date said to be sometime in the ninth century from which it was conjectured that the Church to which they belonged might have been built in or before the Reign of Ethelwulf.

It was dedicated to the Virgin Mary.

Dr. 'Hoadly the present Rector built the Chancel at his own expense and contributed largely towards completing the rest and it is now a very neat structure with a beautiful Tower and a fine Peal of six bells.

The Parsonage House[1] which has been greatly enlarged and improved and indeed almost new built by Dr. Hoadly is now a very handsome building. The garden and outlet adjoining have been also by him very much improved and rendered exceedingly pleasant : in the whole of which a large sum of money must have been expended.

The House stands on the North part of the Church at the distance of about 100 yards. On the East side of the Church yard is the site of the Manor of Old Alresford whereon stands a Mansion House built by Captain Rodney (now Sir George Bridges Rodney Baronet) about the year 1752 ; on the same spot where the ancient Manor House stood : the site and Domains of the Manor being held by him on a lease from the Bishop of Winchester who is Lord of the Manor and Patron of the Rectory. The juries of the Courts Leat and Baron for the Manor are constantly impaneled on a particular spot in a garden belonging to the Manor House after which they adjourn to New Alresford where the rest of the business of the Court is transacted. The Parish or Tything of Medstead being part of the Manor of Old Alresford the tenants are obliged to do suit at the Courts of Alresford when they are warned on the jury, or have business to do respecting their copyholds but they are not obliged to attend the Court for making surrenders, there being several officers before whom surrenders may at any time be made out of Court, *viz.* the Steward of the Bishopric and Clerk of the lands and the Bailiff and Clerk of the Bailiwick of Bishop's Sutton.

[1] Now the residence of Percy Laming, Esq. (1937).

The Steward and Clerk of the Bishopric may take surrenders anywhere but it has been held that the Bailiff and Clerk of the Bailiwick must take them within the Bailiwick unless authorized by special deputation from the Steward or Clerk of the lands. About a mile distant from the Manor House towards the North-east stands another Mansion House built by James Rodney, Esq. about the year 1768 to which great additions are now making by Samuel Rolleston Esq. who lately purchased the same.

The Church and these three houses stand on an eminence fronting the South, having the great Pond and the Town of New Alresford in full view before them : and command a various and delightful prospect over villages and rivulets, fields and meadows, to the Downs and woods on the distant hills.

The great Pond lies within the Parish of Old Alresford although it joins to the Houses of New Alresford on the South-west part.

RECTORS OF OLD ALRESFORD.

THE following is a list of the Rectors of Old Alresford *i.e.* of the united parishes :—

1225. Godfrey de Tostes.
1280. Jordan de Marisco.
1316. John of Heydon.
1339 (July 5). Adam of Wamberghe.
1339 (Oct. 23). John of Nubbeleghe.
        Thomas of Edington.
1354 (Jan. 10). Thomas of Enham.
1361 (June 29). Walter of Sevenhampton.
1370 (Oct. 17). John Turke.
1397 (Sept. 10). Richard Prentys.
        Thomas Forest.
1463 (Sept. 28). David Husband.
1472 (Oct. 22). Henry Eryvin.
1485 (Dec. 19). Brian Holmes.
1501 (May 14). Robert Sherborne.
        Ralph Lexton.

1525. Roger Stokesley.
1558 (Jan.). John Seaton.
1559. William Wakeling.
1575. John Watson, Bishop of Winchester in 1580.
1581. Nicholas Bonde.
1608. George Ryves.
1613. Thomas Moreton.
1616. Dr. Hamlet Marshall.
1653. Dr. Peter Heylin.

    (During Heylin's deposition under Cromwell in 1640 :—
        1640. Thomas Twisse.
        1655. John Allen.
        1656. Roger Moore.
        1659. John Taylor.

    Dr. Heylin was reinstated in 1661, died 1662.)

1662. Dr. George Beaumont, B.D., Prebendary of Winchester.
1687. William Needham, B.D., Prebendary of S. Davids.
1727. Joseph Soley, Prebendary of Winchester.
1737. Dr. John Hoadly, LL.D., Chancellor of Winchester.
1776. Dr. William Buller, D.D., Prebendary of Winchester, afterwards Bishop of Exeter.
1797. Francis North, Earl of Guildford, Prebendary of Winchester.
1850. George Henry Sumner, D.D., subsequently Canon of Winchester, Archdeacon, and Bishop of Guildford.

RECTORS OF OLD ALRESFORD SINCE THE DIVISION OF THE PARISHES.

1886. Sir Frederick Larkins Currie, Bart.
1894. Frederick Matthews Middleton.
1904. George Owen Pardoe.
1913. George Herbert Preston.
1936. Edmund Robert Morgan, Archdeacon of Winchester.

THE MOTHERS' UNION.

THE now world-wide Mothers' Union was founded at Old Alresford by Mary Sumner, wife of the then Rector, George Henry Sumner, afterwards Bishop of Guildford. A tablet to her memory was placed in the Church in 1936.

The inscription on the memorial tablet runs as follows :—

" In thankful remembrance of the life and work of

MARY SUMNER

wife of George Sumner Rector of Old Alresford
1851 and Bishop of Guildford 1888
In 1875 with the help of her husband she founded the
Mothers' Union as a Society to uphold Christian Marriage
and to sanctify the homes of the people
Endowed with special gifts of body mind and soul she was
enabled by the grace of God to quicken and inspire
with her love and zeal the hearts of many in this
great work throughout the world."

A VERY EARLY FIRE.

IN the 7th year of Henry the Second's Reign, Alresford in Hampshire totally burnt 1160.

(From Philip Luckombe's Book of memorable events in History.)

1644.

Duthy, in his *Sketches in Hampshire*, 1839, says :—

" Previously to the battle of Cheriton the town of Alresford was occupied by the Royal troops and became the headquarters of the Earl of Forth and Lord Hopton. After victory had declared in favour of Sir William Waller and the cavaliers were obliged to quit it, they set fire to it at both ends as they retreated ; probably in revenge for the parliamentary politics of some of its principal inhabitants. The fire, however, was soon extinguished, without much damage ensuing, through the exertions of the victorious Roundheads, who came pouring into the place."

E

THE FIRES OF ALRESFORD.

As will be seen from the foregoing records, Alresford has often been the scene of devastating fires. Besides those already mentioned, others have been recorded in the Parish Registers. It may be of interest to gather here the date and extent of each. In view of the fact that Alresford has now a well-equipped Fire Station with two excellent engines and a most efficient Fire Brigade it may be hoped that in the event of future outbreaks of fire the lives and properties of the inhabitants will be well safeguarded.

1160.   7th year of King Henry II. Town totally burnt.

1440.   Half the town was burnt down.

1620.   A great part of West Street was burnt. (Parish Registers.)

1644.   The Royalist troops before marching out set the town on fire at both ends. It was soon extinguished by the Roundheads who pursued them.

1678.   On May Day a fire broke out in West Street. (Parish Registers.)

1689.   The Church, the Market House, and many houses were destroyed by a fire which broke out in three places at once. By it 117 families were made homeless.

1736.   Many houses were burnt on April 30th. (Parish Registers.)

" . . . It burnt ye dwellings of 30 families with all the outhouses, barns and stables to the number of 86 Piles of buildings besides damage 5000 lbs and upwards."

At one time a fire engine was kept in the tower of the Church ; it was admitted by a door on the west of the tower made for that purpose early in the 19th century. Prior to this the only entrance from without was by a small door now blocked up, on the north face of the tower.

THE MARKET HOUSE IN 1774.

THE Market House is far from being a handsome building, and there are two or three mean-looking houses or shops standing in the middle of the market place which are a great desight to the town as well as a newsance to people who travel on the road for they not only cause a kind of winding in the great London Road but intercept part of those delightful prospects which open to the several streets into different quarters for several miles into the country. If all these were taken away it would leave a spacious open square which could not be equalled in many country towns in England. The houses or shops were formerly open shambles used by Butchers before the great fire of 1689 for selling meat in the markets but the owners of them being burnt out of these dwelling houses ran up these erections on the spots where the several shambles had stood, as a temporary shelter till their houses could be rebuilt, and from that time have been suffered to keep them as close private buildings.

There were, some years since, several others besides these that are now standing but being held by leases for 99 years of the Bailiff and Burgesses they were taken down as fast as their several terms expired.

1780.

Bull Baiting at Alresford advertized.

A *gratis* dinner to all who produced a good bull dog.

Prizes : A silver collar to the owner of the dog who pins oftenest, and 7/6 for the second best.

(*Hampshire Chronicle.*)

TRADESMEN'S TOKENS.

Jervas Abin at ye George in Alresford. 1667.
Robert Hockley at ye Bell in Alresford. 1657.

There are 150 examples of Hampshire traders' tokens of the 17th century extant.

1780.

On April 24 a cricket match announced to come off at the New Ground called the Nythe for eleven new hats. The challengers are Alresford eleven : date Whit-monday : and all gentlemen cricketers are notified as to the winning of hats.

(*Hampshire Chronicle.*)

MARY RUSSELL MITFORD.

On December 16th, 1787, Mary Russell Mitford, the well-known author of *Our Village*, was born in Broad Street, Alresford, in a house now known as " Mitford House." Her father, a doctor, removed from Alresford when she was only four years old. The village which she made so famous was not Alresford but Three Mile Cross near Reading.

1792.

The following is an extract from the *Universal British Directory*, 1792 :—

" The Mail Coach from London passes through Alresford every morning between three and four o'clock, and continues its journey to Poole, from which place it arrives every night, about eleven o'clock, at Alresford, on its way to the Bell and Crown Inn, Holborn. The Post Office opens at eight every morning and shuts at nine o'clock at night.

" Collyer's Coach, from Southampton, arrives every day at the Swan Inn to breakfast, and gets to the Bell Savage, Ludgate Hill, every evening at six o'clock ; comes from London every morning to Alresford to dinner at two o'clock, and gets to Southampton by six in the evening ; fare, fifteen shillings from Alresford to London, and five shillings from Alresford to Southampton.

" Besant's Coach, upon a new construction, with eight wheels, sets out from the Swan with two Necks, Lad-Lane, and Golden Cross, Charing Cross, every morning at six o'clock, to and from Southampton, through this town : fare by this coach to London is twelve shillings.

E

Mary Russell Mitford, born 1787 at No.27, Broad Street, Alresford

" Jane Astell's Waggons set out every Sunday and Wednesday evening for London, and return thence to Alresford every Monday and Friday morning and go to Southampton, from whence they return to Alresford every Wednesday and Saturday morning.

" There are also Brookman's Waggons from Southampton to London, pass through Alresford every Monday and Thursday, and return every Tuesday and Friday to Southampton. Carriage of goods from London to Alresford two shillings and ninepence per hundredweight."

WILD LIFE IN ALRESFORD POND IN 1937.

(Kindly supplied by Mr. C. F. G. R. SCHWERDT, of Alresford House.)

THE coarse fish mentioned in the MS. are pike, tench, perch, carp, roach and eels. Of these, perch and carp have disappeared, and trout are only swimming in sheltered places in the two rivers, *i.e.* the river from Bighton and the river going by the Mill.

The largest pike which has been caught in the Pond was about 30lbs., but the fishing is strictly preserved because the present owner could not keep the Pond as an aviary unless he did so. Tench still run up to several pounds, but as they mud the water they are not admired as a sporting fish. Plenty of eels and roach are to be found and are probably affording great food to the pike. Tradition says that several large trout have been caught, but I have been unable to verify this. One trout weighing 16lbs. was caught by a coachman of Lord Rodney, the original owner of the property.

In the many small tributaries, principally tributaries of the river running from Bighton, and which run through the watercress beds, there are quantities of different small fish such as lampreys, miller's thumbs, sticklebacks, and an increasing number of dace.

As a result of the great care which has always been given to the Park and the streams leading into and out of the Pond, I think there is an increase in the kinds of birds which have been observed. I mention the crested grebe, lesser grebe, little grebe or dabchick, water rail, coot, moorhen, pochard widgeon, oyster catcher, tufted duck, bittern, plover, kingfisher, redshank, and lately the greenshank or summer snipe. Cormorants and puffins occasionally struggle over from the Isle of Wight in a storm. Herons unfortunately are increasing because they have started to build in Bighton Wood. There are large flocks of duck and teal. These birds all nest on the Pond and their nests are strictly preserved.

There are millions of starlings since Colonel Hawker's time, who relates in his diary how he shot 243 with one shot on October 26th, 1825, and that two months afterwards another 200 to 300 were found dead in the reeds. Of small birds there is a large quantity, including a great many rarities such as three kinds of reed warbler, two sorts of golden-crested wren, the butcher bird, grey and yellow wagtail and flycatcher.

Occasionally an otter appears, but it cannot be hunted owing to the extent of the marshy land. There are also stoats and weasels, including a brown and white variety, owls, marsh harriers, and several hawks such as the kestrel and sparrow-hawk.

ANCIENT REMAINS. (MS.)

ABOUT a mile west of Alresford on a Hill called Ovington Hill or Burrough Hill (? Burrow Hill) are the remains of a fortified camp partly in Ovington and partly in Tichborne. At what time or on what occasion this fortification was made is uncertain. In 1775 a farmer ploughing in a field within the entrenchment found a piece of coin of fine gold with an inscription.

There is another entrenchment on Fobdown about a mile north of Alresford and about half a mile from the above. Another square camp is in Abbotsdon Down about a mile east of Fobdown with a large Burrow in the middle. Each of these is to be seen from the streets of the Town.

THE DEAN.

IN all old maps and records, the part of Alresford from Perin's School to the river is called " The Dean."

In Cassell's *Encyclopaedia Dictionary*, a dean is defined as a " sandy valley," a " narrow valley."

Mr. T. W. Shore, F.G.S., etc., in the *History of Hampshire*, says : " The limits of the forest land in Hampshire at the settlement of the Saxons can be traced by the numerous names ' dean ' and ' den ' which they give to various localities. These names occur all over the county, such as : Borden, Hatherden, Vernham's Dean, and Toresden near Andover, which relate to the early limits of the forest of Chute. Chidden, Denmead, Horndean and Finchdean refer to the eastern limits of the forest of East Bere : while Longwood Dean and Dean near Bishop's Waltham refer to its western limits.

" Bramdean, Ropley Dean and Derdean are names which relate to the ancient forest of mid-Hampshire. Dean, Deangate, Clyds-dean relate to the northern forest, while Nordens, Highden and Dean near Sparsholt are old boundary names relating to the forest of West Bere."

N.B.—Until quite recent times the spelling Dean has been persistent. The attempt to change it to Dene is surely a mistake.

THE MARKETS OF ALRESFORD.
(From the MS.)

THE markets which are held weekly on Thursday, partly through the situation of the place and partly by the re-establishment of the navigation from Winchester to Southampton, are become very considerable. In times when there is a free exportation of corn, it is one of the greatest markets in Hampshire for Wheat and Barley, and in this respect one of the chief supplies of the navigable river. But the corn is all sold here by sample so that the appearance of the Corn Market is by no means adequate to the business done here in that way.

"The Old Deer House", Brug Green

For in time of exportation although there frequently are above an hundred loads of wheat sold in a day, yet not a single load is brought and pitched in the Market and the country round being famous for excellent barley large quantities of this are also sold here in like manner.

For sheep it is one of the greatest Markets in England especially from Michaelmas to Christmas, not indeed for Hampshire sheep only but large droves are brought out of Dorsetshire, Wiltshire, etc., and sold in these markets to the Farmers, Graziers and Jobers who come every year out of Kent, Surrey, Sussex, Berks, Buckinghamshire and other counties to buy them. The largest of these sheep markets are generally on the first Thursday after Old Michaelmas Day and two Thursdays in November. Two particular market days in the year are distinguished from the ordinary markets. One is that on the first Thursday after Old Michaelmas Day and the other on the next day after Ash Wednesday. The first of these is not only for sheep as before mentioned but also for Horses and other cattle and also for wearing apparel of divers kinds and for toys, haberdashery, seed, wheat and other commodities. The other is for cheese and bacon brought out of the West and for bread, corn and seed barley, oats, pease and grass seeds.

All these markets by the public spirit of the proprietors are at present permitted to be toll free for Bacon, Cheese and all commodities whatsoever except sheep, and such goods are sold on standings furnished by the Clerk of the Market and on some of the great sheep market days, for encouragement of the Markets, no toll is taken for cooping unless the sheep are sold.

Besides the weekly markets there are two annual Fairs, one on Holy Thursday and the other on Old Midsummer Day, the first of these is chiefly for Corn, Sheep, Cows, Calves, Bulls, Horses, Haberdashery and Pedlary wares, the other is not only for these articles, but considerable quantities of Bacon and Cheese have of late years been brought out of the Western Counties and sold here. It has lately been advertised as open and toll free, not only for these but for leather, flour, wool and such other goods, wares and commodities as are usually carried back out of Hampshire into those counties.

Mr. J. Ridley Shield, of Cardew, Alresford, the last to hold the office of Bailiff and for many years Chairman of the Town Trust, kindly supplies the following note which amplifies the MS. account of the government of the Town and Borough (see p. 18) and tells of the origin of the several Fairs by grant of the Bishop of Winchester, Robert Horne (1561—1579).

By a Charter dated the 10th day of December 1573 Robert by Divine Permission Bishop of Winchester seeing that the Borough and Town of New Alresford was in great decay and poverty made the following grant :

He granted for himself and his successors for ever that for the future there shall be within our Town 1 Bailiff and 8 chief Burgesses of the better and more honest inhabitants of the Town to be chosen for the good governance of the Borough.

He then appoints John Heather Bailiff from the date of the grant until the Feast-day of St. Michael the Archangel next and until our other Burgesses be chosen. The 8 Burgesses were appointed to be in office so long as they behaved themselves and he granted the Burgesses the right to elect a Burgess yearly.

There follow instructions how the post of Bailiff is to be filled if he die during his year of office.

Then he grants to the Bailiff and Burgesses and their successors the right to hold a Fair at New Alresford yearly on the Feast of the Ascension (sheep) and also a Fair on the Feast-day of St. John (pleasure), also a free market every week on Thursday (this has been done away with long ago).

Also all commodities and rights whatsoever and profits from the same and the goods and chattels, felons and fugitives taken and strayed within the Town and Borough of New Alresford ; certain rights over bread, beer and wine, and right to put a baker in the pillory and a brewer in the tumbrel or pillory. The Bailiff and Burgesses are to pay to the Bishop and his successors the rent of £15. 15s. 6¼d. at the Feast of S. Michael in every year.

The Bailiff and Burgesses were done away with by Lord Rosebery's " Municipal Corporations Act " of 1883 and Town Trustees were appointed in 1896 to take their place under a scheme drawn up by the Charity Commissioners.

The rent has now to be paid to the Charity Commissioners.

The Avenue on Pound Hill and the verge on the opposite side of the road now belong to the Town Trustees.

ALRESFORD SHEEP FAIR.

THE following interesting statistics have been obtained by Mr. J. R. Shield from the office of the *Hampshire Chronicle.*

In recent years the sheep penned at Alresford Fair have averaged about 8000. In July 1937 the number was stated to be 10,000, an increase of 3000 on the year before (1936 fell below the average). In the year 1885 it is recorded that 20,000 were penned, though trade was the worst for many years owing to long-continued drought. In 1886 about 15,000 sheep were penned at the Fair ; in 1887 the return is given as " about 1400 less than last year " ; in 1888 the number was about the same as in 1887 ; in 1889 the words in the *Chronicle* report are " an average number of about 16,000." It would therefore seem as if the number of sheep had gone down one half in 50 years.

On reference to the *Hampshire Chronicle* of 100 years ago it is found that in 1837 the sheep penned at the Fair numbered about 140,000 : that the " Corporation of Alresford " then presented a five-guinea cup for competition, and that " a liberal subscription was entered into by yeomanry and farmers to present Mr. Henry Dancaster with a handsome piece of plate for his exertions in promoting the interests of the Fair."

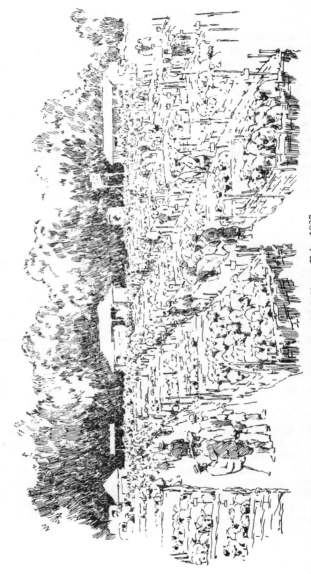

Alresford Sheep Fair, 1937
H. Hodgson

It is almost remarkable that Alresford Fair should have kept going, when so many of these old Hampshire Sheep Fairs have disappeared altogether.

In this immediate neighbourhood, Overton may be particularly mentioned. Of that Fair, which used to precede Alresford, it was reported in 1886 that the number of sheep penned was 22,000, or 8000 less than the year before, and that " within the memory of living persons as many as 75,000 were to be seen on the ground." Times have changed ; weekly markets and repository sales have largely superseded annual Fairs.

THE GREAT WAR. 1914—1918.

FOR the following account of Alresford during the War, I am indebted to Mr. E. Jesty, Headmaster of the Dean Elementary School, who for his work in the National Savings Campaign was awarded the Order of the British Empire (M.B.E.).

" The outbreak of hostilities in August 1914 brought great changes to Alresford, and before the end of the year the town had become a military centre. In December a battalion of Argyll and Sutherland Highlanders and a further battalion of Royal Scotch Fusiliers were billeted here. To accommodate these extra men—more than the original population—it was necessary to place them in practically every household, whilst barns, sheds, outbuildings, and the local Council Schools were requisitioned, the children attending the latter being granted three months holiday. Having completed their training, the battalions left for France, and they were succeeded by battalions of the Gordon Highlanders and Cameron Highlanders, the latter regiment being in charge of Cameron of Lochiel.

" It is of interest to note that Ian Hay (Major Beith) wrote his popular novel *The First Hundred Thousand* whilst billeted at St. Joan's, Alresford, and that the old and original Perin's School on the opposite side of the road was used as Battalion's Headquarters and Guard Room.

" In addition to troops for active service, members of the Royal Defence Corps were also stationed in the town for the purpose of guarding the railway, bridges, etc., and these included members of the London Territorials and the Durham Light Infantry. A volunteer section, consisting of men who were not eligible for active service, was also formed locally.

" In the town itself the call for recruits was responded to by many who were eager to join Kitchener's Army. Under the Derby Scheme large numbers joined the Forces, and the town had a long list of men serving in the various branches of His Majesty's Forces, a record of these being kept and posted in the Parish Church. Many never returned, and the Memorial to the fallen on the south wall of the Parish Church contains no less than 54 names of those who made the supreme sacrifice. This Memorial was erected by public subscription.

"Another Memorial to the memory of the fallen was erected in the churchyard near the west door, and was the gift of Mr. H. H. Walford, of Arle Bury, and takes the form of a granite cross placed in a small Garden of Remembrance.

" When the Belgians were forced to evacuate their own country, some of the refugees came to Alresford, where a house in West Street was handed over to them, the same building having been previously used as the headquarters for fifty " conscientious objectors."

"At the local garage, machinery was installed for making munition shells, and a number of women and girls was kept busily engaged on this important work.

" Food economy campaigns were conducted, whilst rationing of certain foods was in general force, the local office being situated in Broad Street. National Saving Associations sprang up in the town and did excellent work and during one week in July, 1918, the sum of £16,08 was saved in Government Securities as the result of special effort in the rural area. For this success the Government named one of its aeroplanes 'Alresford,' but the machine was brought down by the enemy during operation in France."

THE MEMORIAL IN THE PARISH CHURCH.

" To the glorious memory of the men of Alresford who made the supreme sacrifice in the Great War 1914—1918. This Memorial is erected by their fellow townsmen who acknowledge with pride and lasting gratitude all that has been gained by their patriotic devotion."

Aslett, Thomas Henry,
  Pte., 1st Wiltshire Regt.
Baldwin, Henry Will,
  Pte., 1st Somerset Lt. Inf.
Baker, Kingsley (M.C.),
  Lieut., R.F.A.
Benham, James Mac,
  L.-Cpl., 2nd Wiltshire Regt.
Benham, Arthur Thomas,
  Pte., 9th Devons.
Bennett, Victor E. E.,
  Pte., R.M.L. Infantry.
Blake, Francis Henry,
  Rfn., Rifle Brigade.
Blake, William Henry,
  Pte., 1st Hants Regt.
Chown, Albert Henry,
  Pte., 1/5 Devonshire Regt.
Clarke, James Olliver,
  Pte., 1/4 Hants Regt.
Collister, Robert H.,
  Pte., 6th Somerset Lt. Inf.
Cousens, George E.,
  2nd Lieut., Middlesex Regt.
Cromie, Maurice,
  Lt., 3rd Hants (Attd. 2nd Bn.).
Cromie, Henry Julian,   •
  Cpt., 3rd Hants (Attd. 2nd Bn.)
Curtis, Will J. (D.C.M.),
  Sergt., 26th Field Coy., R.E.
Eacher, C.,
  Cpl., 1st Norfolk Regt.
Etheridge, Fred C.,
  Signaller, R.G.A.
Etheridge, W. George,
  Pte., East Surrey Regt.
Gardner, Leonard G.,
  Pte., 12th Hants Regt.
Gardiner, Percy William,
  Pte., Wiltshire Regt.

Gibbs, Richard Will,
  Sapper, R.E.
Giles, David,
  Rfn., 9th Rifle Brigade.
Godwin, Edward,
  Pte., Labour Company.
Grainger, C. E. G.,
  L.-Cpl., 2nd Wiltshire Regt.
Grinham, P. R. J.,
  Lieut., 4/10 Middlesex Regt.
Hazelgrove, H. Chas.,
  Rfn., 18th K.R.R.
Hockley, J.,
  Rfn., Rifle Brigade.
Hodgson, Edward,
  Midshipman, R.N.,
    H.M.S. *Invincible*.
Hodgson, John,
  Lieut., 2nd Dorset Regt.
Jackson, W. H.,
  Pte., 3rd Dorset Regt.
Johnson, Ernest R.,
  C.-Q.-M.-S., 7th K.R.R.
Kersley, Leonard,
  L.-Cpl., King's Own Scottish
    Borderers.
Lee, Alexander C. L.,
  Corpl., 1st K.R.R.
Light, John,
  Rfn., London Rifle Brigade.
Lock, C. F.,
  Pte., 1st Hants Regt.
Marriner, Edward,
  Pte., Somerset Lt. Inf.
Marshall, Walter D.,
  Rfn., 1/16 Q. Westminster Rfs.
Mathias, E. M.,
  Pte., 17th Royal Welsh Fus.
Merritt, Frank,
  Signalman, H.M.S. *Vindictive*.

Mitchell, N.,
  L.-Corpl., K.R.R.
Money, Fred,
  Pte., 2nd Wiltshire Regt.
Money, William,
  Pte., 1st Gloucester Regt.
Munday, Jack G.,
  Pte., R.M.L. Infantry.
Munday, Percy V.,
  Pte., Durham Lt. Infantry.
Newman, Herbert E.,
  Pte., 6th Wiltshire Regt.
Pring, H. F. D.
  Pte., Artists' Rifles.
Shield, Clement R. (M.C.),
  Capt., H.L.I., G.S.O. 3,
    51st Div.

Shirfield, A. R.,
  Gun., 20th Res. Battery, R.F.A.
Smith, Albert J.,
  Pte., 1st Wiltshire Regt.
Wansborough, J. E.,
  Sergt., 9th Field Coy., R.E.
Westbrook, Alfred T.,
  L.-Corpl., 8th City of London
    Regt.
White, William Thos.,
  Pte., 1/5 Gloucester Regt.
Woodward, A.,
  Coy.-Sergt.-Major, 1/4 Hants
    Regt.
Edwards, F. James,
  Pte., 2nd Hants
    (Attd. 88th M.G.C.).

ALRESFORD IN 1937.

ALRESFORD is still a beauty spot set amidst beautiful surroundings. Its wide main street flanked on either side by cobbled banks, Broad Street still wider at right angles to it sloping gently down to the great weir, planted with shady trees ; its approach from the west beside a great avenue of limes and elms, all give it a character peculiarly its own. But it is changing day by day and changing quickly. Old small-paned windows give place to plate-glass shop fronts ; old porticoes are being replaced by modern doors ; the coaching inns of former days are shorn of their glory, and garages and petrol pumps are much more prominent to the eye. A horse is a rare sight and a carriage and pair a memory of the past : a stream of motors rushes through the streets, often constituting, especially in the holiday seasons, a positive danger to pedestrians. Motor transport is indeed to-day a most powerful dis-integrator. It has affected and is affecting life in all directions. Private cars, tradesmen's vans, motor omnibuses and motor lorries carrying heavy goods day and night are changing alike the customs and habits of the people. Godfrey de Lucy's barges afforded a means of carrying Alresford's products to Southampton and so into all the world. They have passed. Improved roads brought

Alresford into nearer touch with county, with cities and with ports ; and great teams of powerful horses drawing waggons, the horse carriages of the well-to-do and mail coaches took their place. Alresford and its inhabitants had constant news of the outer world : its more adventurous sons had the means of travel ever near, and its trade though diminished was active. With the advent of the railways in 1865 came the dawning of yet another era, new markets for perishable goods were opened up, hours not days separated Alresford from London, and at least occasional travel at comparatively small cost was within the reach of all. Alresford's cress beds supplied the town markets and throve exceedingly. They are still thriving and form a chief industry to-day when wool and hides are no longer seen or thought of. Milk in large quantities brought in from surrounding farms could be delivered in London at an early hour. Milk still goes up to London daily, but the railway too seems to have had its day. Now is the day of roads and of motor traffic. Huge lorries shake the quiet streets of Alresford by night : milk is collected by lorries from the farms. Alresford is no longer a shopping centre ; if the tradesmen of Alresford are still dealt with by the country houses in the neighbourhood, the orders can be given by telephone and the goods delivered by motor vans. Even the telephone can be dispensed with, for the orders are solicited by motor and the goods delivered later, while much of the small retail trade is done not in Alresford at all, but by motors carrying the goods for sale to the houses and cottages of the villages around. It is a continual struggle for existence ; the smaller tradesmen are squeezed by the multiple shopping firms, and all in the country are seriously affected by the towns—Winchester and Southampton and elsewhere, easily reached by private cars and by motor. 'buses running at frequent intervals, where with the advantages of shopping can be combined an outing and a visit to the ' Pictures.'

The motor transport facilities do not only affect trade. It was largely due to them that Perin's Grammar School came to its end as a secondary school. Boarding houses were no longer needed when the children could come and return by omnibus. More, there was no longer the need for a secondary school so near to Winchester when Winchester was so easily accessible by train or 'bus.

Perin's Grammar School passed as a secondary school. It is now a senior elementary school. Motor transport has had also a say in that. Children over 11 are brought in from the surrounding villages by omnibus to Perin's. That again has affected village life. Whatever the older children may gain in the way of a better education in a senior school, there can be no doubt but that the junior schools still left in the villages no longer take the place they have occupied so long in the village life. The children of the village are divided in their interests, and the school is no longer the centre in which children and parents alike carry on the school traditions of the past, but is instead a stepping-stone to the habits and manners of the towns.

Motor transport too has affected the religious life of the community. No doubt there are many causes for the increasing neglect of religious ordinances and for infrequent attendance at a place of worship, but there can be no question that very prominent among them is the facility which motor transport affords for getting about the country. Sunday is a day for visits from friends or for paying visits to those who otherwise could not be seen except at long intervals. The seaside is within easy reach by car, and excursions by train or 'bus are provided Sunday by Sunday in the summer. " The old order changeth, yielding place to new." For weal or for woe Alresford is changing fast. The population according to the census of 1921 was 1709 ; according to the census of 1931 it has decreased by 85. Yet new houses are being built continually. Many of these are to supply the place of those condemned recently as insanitary and unfit for habitation. That is all to the good, for though we may be sorry to see the picturesque reminders of the past disappear, yet human happiness and physical fitness are of more value than picturesqueness. But the real meaning of the decrease in population seems to lie in the smaller size of modern families and the absence of children, which is by no means so much a matter for satisfaction ; and while picturesqueness is certainly not everything and comfort and moderate rentals are certainly things to be desired, perhaps a lover of the picturesque may be allowed to deplore the character of so many of the houses now being added and dotted about in all directions, devoid of any pretence of beauty whatever and a serious blot upon the landscape.

Alresford no doubt has a future in store for it. When the private roads are taken over by the District Authority, and the new drainage scheme, at last well upon its way, is accomplished, the population will in all probability increase and it may become a well-ordered, thriving place of residence combining the pleasant amenities of a rural district with the advantages of a country town ; but it seems little likely that it will ever be what it was in the past, a centre of industry and supply, a self-contained and self-supporting community taking any sort of lead among the villages which lie about it.